The Ocean at the End of the Lane

Classroom Questions

A SCENE BY SCENE TEACHING GUIDE

Amy Farrell

SCENE BY SCENE
ENNISKERRY, IRELAND

Scene by Scene
11 Millfield, Enniskerry
Wicklow, Ireland.
www.scenebysceneguides.com

The Ocean at the End of the Lane Classroom Questions/Amy Farrell. —1st ed.
ISBN 978-1-910949-28-3

Contents

Preface

Questions

1. What did Lettie Hempstock say about the duckpond?

2. What does the phrase "the old country" make you think of?

3. What information do you learn about Lettie here?

4. What questions do you have after reading this page?

Prologue

Summary

Following a funeral service, the speaker goes for a drive. Without planning to, he goes to his childhood home and notes how it has changed. He feels disconnected from his past and his younger self.

He knows he has to drive to his sister's house and make small talk about his life with people he has not seen in years.

Instead of doing this, he continues driving away from the town and down the lane of his childhood.

He arrives at the Hempstocks' farm and talks with Mrs Hempstock, who remembers him as Lettie's friend. Then he walks out to the duckpond, where he sits down and begins to remember.

Questions

1. What is the speaker doing as the prologue begins?

2. What makes the speaker keep going when he realises his destination no longer exists?

3. Describe the countryside as the speaker drives down the lane towards the Hempstocks' farmhouse.

4. Does the speaker have a good memory? Support your view.

5. Why did the speaker visit the Hempstocks' farm, in your opinion?

6. What details do you learn about the speaker and his life in this prologue?

Chapter I

Summary

The speaker recalls that nobody came to his seventh birthday, which he then spent alone, reading in his room. He got a black kitten, Fluffy, as a gift from his father, that he loved dearly.

A month later, the cat was run over when the opal miner came to stay. This man replaced the kitten with an unfriendly ginger tomcat. The speaker's family didn't seem to care about the kitten's death, or understand why he should be upset about it.

Questions

1. "Nobody came to my seventh birthday party."
    What is your reaction to this line?

2. "The cake had a book drawn on it, in icing."
    When you read this, what conclusions do you draw about
    the speaker?

3. "They were not my friends, after all."
    Do you feel sorry for the speaker?

4. What happened to Fluffy, the kitten?

5. What do you think of the way the opal miner breaks the
    news about the kitten to the speaker?

6. Describe the new cat. Is he a suitable replacement?

7. "When my parents got home that evening, I do not think
    my kitten was even mentioned."
    What is your reaction to this?

Chapter II

Summary

The speaker recalls that he wasn't a happy child and used to escape from his life in books.

He remembers how life changed when his parents were no longer wealthy and he had to give up his bedroom, sharing instead with his little sister, while his room was rented out to tenants.

On the first day of the spring holidays, while looking for a comic, the speaker discovers that their car has been stolen. The police report that it has been abandoned at the end of the lane, so the speaker and his father walk down to it.

They discover a dead man in the back seat of the car, the opal miner. While police are dealing with the situation, the speaker goes with Lettie, a girl from the farmhouse, so he won't be in the way.

In the farmhouse he is given fresh milk to drink and porridge and jam to eat, and he is happy.

Lettie's mother comes in and talks about the dead man. She knows what he did and why he killed himself. Lettie knows the contents of his suicide note.

Lettie brings the speaker out to her ocean, the duckpond. They find a fish that died from eating a sixpence coin. Lettie tells the speaker that his father is wondering where he is, so they return inside. Lettie tells the boy to keep the sixpence.

His father, the doctor and policeman are in the Hempstocks' kitchen when they return. The police drive them home and the boy's father asks him not to talk about what happened with his sister. The speaker puts the sixpence into his china piggy-bank.

Questions

1. Why was the speaker sorry to give up his bedroom?

2. What is it like, sharing a room with his sister?

3. What is your reaction to the speaker's fear of the dark?

4. What does the speaker discover when he goes looking for his comic?

5. Why does the speaker wish his family would buy normal, white, sliced bread?

6. Describe the lane the police car drives down.

7. What are the policeman's thoughts on who stole the car?

8. What do they discover in the backseat of the car?

9. What seems to have happened to the man?

10. Describe the body in the backseat.

11. What does the speaker's memory about his father and burnt toast, reveal about the speaker and his father?

12. Describe the girl from the farmhouse.

13. Does the speaker like the fresh milk and porridge he's given?

14. Does anything about Lettie or her mother strike you as strange?

15. What powers do they seem to possess?

16. What is unusual about the dead fish?

17. The boy's father asks him not to "talk about this to your sister."
    Does this surprise you?

18. What is the boy's interpretation of the morning's events?

19. What does he do with the sixpence?

20. What are your first impressions of Lettie and her family?

21. What information do we learn about the speaker in this chapter?

Chapter III

Summary

After a day where the speaker wins twenty five pounds on the Premium Bonds and the gardener unearths a bottle of coins, the speaker dreams of being chased and held down by his grandfather and a group of old men. In the dream they force something down his throat and he wakes up, choking on a shilling.

His sister accuses him of throwing coins at her and her friends in the garden.

Lettie Hempstock is waiting for him and he goes with her. She explains that 'something' wants people to have money and says that the opal miner's death has stirred something up. She tells him about the strange and unsettling money related dreams of his neighbours before they have a breakfast of pancakes in the Hempstocks' kitchen.

The speaker realises that the Hempstocks are much older than they seem and somehow know a lot about whatever it is that's going on.

Lettie's mother says they will need a hazel wand for what they must do next. Although Old Mrs Hempstock advises against it, Lettie decides to take the speaker along with her.

Questions

1. What news does the speaker receive in his letter?

2. What does the speaker view his Premium Bonds in terms of?
   Does this tell you anything about him?

3. What does Mr Wollery find in the garden?

4. Describe the speaker's dream.

5. There is something in the boy's throat when he wakes up. What is going on here? What is your reaction to this?

6. Are you surprised that the object in his throat is a coin? Explain your answer.

7. "I wanted to tell someone about the shilling, but I did not know who to tell."
   What makes it difficult for the boy to tell someone?
   What does this tell you about his parents?

8. What does his sister accuse him of?

9. How does Lettie explain what's happening?

10. Would you be scared, if you were the boy?

11. What does Old Mrs Hempstock tell them about the shilling?

12. What have you learned or figured out about Lettie and Old Mrs Hempstock in this chapter?

13. Does the boy like being with the Hempstocks? Explain your point of view.

14. What details does Old Mrs Hempstock refer to that show her great age?

15. What does Lettie's mother say they will need?

16. What does Old Mrs Hempstock tell Lettie to do at the end of the chapter?

17. What do you think could be going on here?

18. What is your reaction to the chapter's last line?

Chapter IV

Summary

Lettie strips a hazel wand and the children track the 'something' that has been causing trouble.

It realises that they are coming after it and tries to repel them. A Manta wolf flies above them, before disappearing into the woods.

Lettie's wand begins to smoulder and burn after she tries to use the boy's coin to amplify its signal.

She warns him to hold her hand, no matter what, and they keep going through a strange, eerie landscape that she says is still part of the Hempstock farm.

They discover what he thinks is a huge tent at first, a giant fabric mask, ripped and torn. This grey thing says it gave the money to help people and Lettie tells it to leave people alone.

The creature won't reveal its name to Lettie, so she starts to bind it as a nameless thing, speaking and singing in an ancient tongue.

Something the size of a football, made of flapping cobwebs and rotting cloth, hurtles at them and the boy catches it, feeling a stabbing pain in his foot as he does so. Lettie knocks it to the ground and grabs his hand again, singing all the while. She binds the creature to that place and they walk home.

He pulls a furry tendril from the earth and finds a kitten, but Lettie advises him not to take it home as it is from this other place. He tells her about his kitten getting knocked down and she sympathises.

She lets go of his hand and they're back on the lane. She tells him that if she had known what they were up against, she wouldn't have brought him along. Lettie also remarks that she wishes he hadn't let go of her hand.

Questions

1.   Describe the scene in the hazel thicket.

2.   What does Lettie do with the hazel wand?

3.   How does the speaker feel, holding Lettie's arm?
     How would you feel in his position?

4.   Is Lettie brave here?

5.   What strange creature do they encounter in the woods?
     Describe its appearance.

6.   What is the atmosphere like as the children pursue the
     Manta wolf through the dark forest?

7.   How has the landscape changed?
     What, do you think, is going on here?

8.   What 'being' do they encounter?

9.   What does it tell them?

10. How does the boy feel in the presence of the grey thing?

11. "I'll bind you as a nameless thing."
     How does Lettie 'bind' the creature?
     What happens, as she binds it?

12. What happens when he lets go of Lettie's hand?

13.   What is the 'language of shaping'?

        When in his life has the speaker understood it?

14.   What is the effect of Lettie's binding?

15.   Describe the landscape as they walk back to the farm.

16.   What does he find when the boy pulls a "furry tendril" from the earth?

        Why won't Lettie let him take it home?

17.   Does Lettie think their encounter with the grey thing went well?

18.   What picture are you forming of Lettie and her abilities?

19.   What interests you in the story so far?

20.   From what we have read, how can you explain the Hempstocks' abilities?

Chapter V

Summary

The boy examines the sole of his foot and discovers a hole with a worm in it. He goes to the bathroom and uses a tweezers and scalding hot water to remove most of it. He puts the worm down the drain and covers the hole in his foot with a sticking plaster.

He accepts the worm in his foot as normal, just one of those things, and is not scared by it. He goes back to his room and reads a Secret Seven mystery, once his sister has fallen asleep.

Questions

1.   What does the boy find when he examines the sole of his foot?

    What is your reaction to this?

2.   Why doesn't he ask an adult for help?

    Do you understand where he's coming from?

3.   Why isn't the boy scared by what's happening?

    Would you be frightened in his position?

4.   How does he get the worm out of his foot?

5.   Describe the piece of worm he removes.

6.   "I wondered, as I wondered so often when I was that age, who *I* was..." Describe the boy's personality, based on what we have read so far.

7.   Do you think this is the end of the matter with the worm in his foot?

Chapter VI

Summary

The boy's mother has a new job, so a new housekeeper and childminder, Ursula Monkton, has come to stay.

The boy's sister adores her immediately, but he is wary of her. Despite her pretty appearance, she reminds him of the grey thing he encountered with Lettie.

Ursula prevents him from going to see Lettie, magically appearing just as he attempts to sneak away. She tells him that she has been inside him, and that nobody will believe him if he tries to tell someone about her.

He realises that she is connected to the worm he found in his foot. He feels he is responsible for her being here. He tries to phone Lettie, but Ursula comes on the line and blocks him.

He doesn't eat any dinner, as Ursula prepared it. He sneaks downstairs to the television room after bedtime, to talk to his father. Ursula is in the television room though, and she sends him back to bed.

Questions

1.   Why is the boy's mother happy?

2.   Why is Ursula coming to stay with them?

3.   Why does the speaker enjoy reading so much?

4.   Why does he like myths?

5.   How does the boy react when he meets Ursula?

6.   Does his sister like Ursula?

7.   "Ursula Monkton was my fault, I was certain of it."
      Why does the boy feel responsible here?
      Do you think he is right to feel this way?

8.   What stops the boy from eating the sandwiches that
      Ursula made?

9.   What differences does the author note between children
      and adults? Is he accurate here, in your view?

10.   How is the boy prevented from going to the Hempstock
      farm?
      What, do you think, is going on here?

11. What supernatural powers does Ursula have?

12. Is Ursula a threatening figure?

13. "If you tell anybody anything, they won't believe you." What is your reaction to Ursula's arrival in their home?

14. Why doesn't the boy eat his dinner?

15. What keeps him awake that night?

16. Why does *Mission: Impossible* make him uneasy?

17. Why doesn't the boy tell his parents what's happening?

Chapter VII

Summary

The next day, the boy's father comes home from work early and shows Ursula Monkton around the gardens. They seem very comfortable together. The boy is afraid to go over to his father, in case it makes him angry.

He sees his father touch Ursula's bottom, but doesn't understand what this means.

Later, he refuses to eat his dinner, calling Ursula a monster. He runs away from his father and locks himself in the bathroom.

His father follows him upstairs and breaks the bathroom door down, before trying to drown the boy in the bath.

Clinging on to his father's tie with his hands and teeth is what saves him.

Afterwards, his father seems unmoved. He tells his son to be grateful that his mother's not home, and sends him to his room.

Questions

1. How does Ursula control the boy?
    What is your reaction to this?

2. "She laughed at all his jokes."
    What is Ursula doing to manipulate the boy's father?

3. What stops the boy from running over to his father?

4. "I was terrified of him when he was angry."
    Does the boy have a good relationship with his father?

5. Why doesn't the boy react when he sees his father place
    his hand on Ursula's bottom? What is going on here?

6. Why does the boy get in trouble at dinner?
    Could he have done anything differently here?

7. Were you surprised when the boy's father broke the
    bathroom door?

8. Why is his sister whimpering, in your opinion?

9. How do you feel as his father fills the bath with cold water?

10. How does the boy save himself?

11. After almost drowning him, his father accuses the boy of
    ruining his tie and sends him to his room. What is your
    reaction to this?

12. Can you think of any reason to explain why his father is behaving like this?

13. What would you do next, in the boy's position?

Chapter VIII

Summary

The boy, wet and cold, is confined to his room, alone. His sister is to sleep in with their parents. Ursula takes away the matches to prevent him from having a fire to warm and dry himself. He is locked in his bedroom as part of his punishment.

He cries until he is all cried out and then decides to try to escape. He reasons that Ursula will not expect him to attempt an escape, so there is a chance he will succeed this time.

He climbs down a drainpipe, past the empty television room. He looks into the drawing room through a crack in the curtains, and sees his father having sex with Ursula. He doesn't fully understand what he's seeing, but is glad that Ursula is busy, and so unlikely to catch him.

He heads for Lettie Hempstock's, leaving the road and running through fields, for fear his father and Ursula are after him.

The boy loses track of where exactly he's headed, but does his best to keep moving in the direction of the farm. The rain falls harder and strange lightning lights up the sky.

He sees a space in the hedge, but then hears Ursula's voice. He turns to see her floating in the air above him.

As he runs away, she taunts him, saying she'll lock him in the attic and have his father drown him every night, until she tires of him. She says she'll bring her friends to the attic and he'll never have books or stories again. He falls to the ground, exhausted, wetting himself in fear.
As Ursula descends, he sees a kitten and picks it up. Stroking the kitten, he says he won't go with Ursula.

Lettie appears and takes the boy's hand. Ursula, wreathed in swirling lightning, is unconcerned when Lettie tells her to get off her land. She tells Lettie that she has waited for her chance to walk the true Earth and will take all she wants from our world. She demands the speaker, saying she owns him.

Lettie tells Ursula to go away once more and holds the boy tightly. The field begins to glow and Ursula rises into the air as Lettie whispers old words. Ursula is swept away into the night, although there is no wind.

Lettie brings the boy home to warm him up. He's afraid that because Lettie didn't kill Ursula, she will come back again.

Lettie tells him that the kitten is the same one from the time they encountered the grey thing.

The boy tells Lettie he doesn't want to go home. What he wants is his home as it was before the miner's death, before things changed.

Questions

1.   What state is the boy in after the episode in the bathtub?

2.   What does Ursula do next to further isolate him?

3.   "She would not expect me to leave now."
        Is the boy brave here, or desperate?

4.   Where did the boy learn to climb down drainpipes?
        Does this surprise you?

5.   Why does he keep thinking that he's in bed?
        What is going on here?

6.   "I was not sure what I was looking at."
        What is going on with his father and Ursula Monkton?
        Does this surprise you?

7.   What makes the boy leave the road?

8.   Describe the storm. How does it add to the atmosphere?

9.   Is the scene with Ursula floating above him
        frightening? Explain your view.

10.   How does Ursula taunt and threaten the boy?

11.   "She was the storm, she was the lightning, she was the
        adult world with all its power and all its secrets and all its
        foolish casual cruelty."
        Comment on this.

12. What makes the boy feel braver?

13. How does Lettie get rid of Ursula Monkton?

14. When the boy says he doesn't want to go home, what does he really mean?

15. Were you expecting Lettie to save the speaker? Explain your view.

Chapter IX

Summary

The Hempstock women prepare a hot bath in their kitchen for the boy and feed him soup to warm him.

He feels safe and at ease, despite the peculiar circumstances, as he eats and bathes and has his clothes mended.

Lettie gives him a white nightgown to wear and he has a roast beef dinner with them.

Old Mrs Hempstock announces that his parents are coming, and he fears he'll be brought home and locked in the attic until Ursula lets his father kill him. Lettie's mother assures him this won't happen, but he isn't convinced.

Old Mrs Hempstock magically smooths things over with the boy's parents. She performs a 'snip and stitch', freezing his parents and cutting out a piece of the boy's dressing gown, that somehow removes his father's memory of the bathtub incident. She sews the edges of his dressing gown back together and his parents unfreeze. They are a little confused and agree to let the boy stay the night, believing they were dropping his toothbrush up to him.

When his parents leave, Old Mrs Hempstock gives the boy the cut-out scrap of fabric, telling him that it is his evening. She advises him to burn it. He hesitates at first, afraid he'll forget the evening's events, but then he throws it on the flames.

As it burns he remembers his father's attempts to drown him. He falls to the floor with intense pain in his foot and discomfort in his chest.

Ginnie examines the hole in his foot and he explains about the worm that was inside it.

Old Mrs Hempstock asks him to be brave, something he doubts he can do. Then she reaches down with her sewing needle and stabs it into the hole in his foot.

She twists and pulls something out of him. He feels it leaving his leg, groin, stomach and chest. It is a long, thin, hole, which they place in a jam jar once it is removed. This hole was what the flea intended to use to get home, this was why she wanted to take the boy back to his attic.

The Hempstocks are happy to have the flea's way home.

Lettie leads the boy to his room, accompanied by the kitten. Although there is still a monster at home in his house, the kitten helps him to sleep.

Questions

1. How do Lettie, her mother and Old Mrs Hempstock look after the boy?

2. How does he feel in the Hempstocks' kitchen?

3. Do you notice anything significant about the food he has with the Hempstocks?

4. What do you learn about the Hempstock men?

5. How does Mrs Hempstock know the boy's parents are coming?

6. What does the boy fear will happen when his parents bring him home?

7. What suggestions do the women make, to help the boy go undiscovered?

8. "And if they are being controlled by the flea, she'll just feed the franticness." According to Lettie, how are his parents being influenced by Ursula?

9. "I had not told them about the bathtub. I did not wonder how she knew."
   The Hempstocks appear to know the impossible and somehow control matters that should be out of their control. What is going on here, in your opinion?

10.   How do the Hempstocks smooth things over with the boy's parents?

11.   The incident with the bathtub was horrible, but the boy wants to remember it. Why?
        Can you appreciate why he feels this way?

12.   What happens to the boy when he throws the scrap of cloth on to the fire?

13.   What does Old Mrs Hempstock do to the hole in his foot with her needle?

14.   Describe what she removes from his foot.
        What is your reaction to this?

15.   'I'm sorry I let go of your hand, Lettie.'
        Does Lettie make him feel bad about what happened?

16.   What does the boy notice about the moon, as he follows Lettie up to bed? What is going on here?

17.   How does the boy feel, as the chapter ends?

18.   Do you trust the Hempstocks? Give reasons for your opinion.

Chapter X

Summary

The boy wakes up, troubled by nightmares he can't remember and wishes he could go back to yesterday, before Ursula Monkton and all the upset in the bathtub.

He gets up, uses the chamber pot, and sees a full, orange moon outside. Old Mrs Hempstock is walking up and down with a staff, and seeing her comforts the boy.

He sleeps soundly until morning. He gets up, washes his hands and face, and dresses in some old-fashioned clothes that have been laid out for him. Then he follows the kitten downstairs, after first taking a wrong turn because the house's layout appears altered since the night before.

Ginnie Hempstock greets him at the bottom of the stairs. Lettie has gone on an errand to fetch things she may need to get rid of Ursula Monkton.

The boy enjoys breakfast before Lettie arrives.

Lettie returns looking miserable, with a scratched and bloody cheek. She has had a difficult time, getting things she may need to deal with Ursula.

The boy looks into her shopping bag to see lots and lots of broken toys. Lettie adds the jam jar containing the wormhole to her collection.

She tells the boy he doesn't have to come with her while she goes to talk to Ursula, but he wants to, saying he'll feel safer with her, something Lettie doesn't look happy about.

They go outside and sit by Lettie's ocean and the boy talks to her about her family and what they really are. They talk about monsters and Ursula Monkton, and wonder what she is scared of.

The boy thinks that grown-ups and monsters aren't scared of anything, but Lettie says there are no real grown-ups, on the inside they look as they always have.

The boy says her ocean is just a pond and Lettie defends it, saying it is as big as necessary. Then she tells him that she knows what Ursula fears, that she fears it too. She doesn't tell him exactly what this fearful thing is though.

They go back inside and the boy looks for reassurance from Lettie that she won't let Ursula get him. Then they walk home to his house together.

Lettie walks around the boy's garden, burying objects from her shopping bag to stop the flea leaving.

Although the boy doesn't understand what Lettie is doing and feels she doesn't explain things fully, he trusts her completely. He doesn't feel scared at all, such is his belief in Lettie and her abilities.

When they go in, his sister is playing the piano. She is confused by his not being in trouble anymore and by his staying the night with a friend, when he doesn't have any friends.

Lettie places an object on each step as they go up to Ursula's room. She is lying naked on the bed. Grey strips, like bandages, hang from the ceiling and the room seems to lilt and sway like a ship.

Ursula tells Lettie that she has no intention of going home, that she is the only one of her kind and that people can't defend themselves against her. Because of this, she is enjoying herself in the boy's home, and intends to stay.

Ursula is not afraid of Lettie, calling her foolish for attempting to bind her without knowing her name.

Lettie produces the jam jar with the wormhole, offering it to Ursula, saying that although they can't get her home, they'll make her safe somewhere similar to it.

The grey cloth strips detach from the ceiling and move in on Lettie and the boy. They attach themselves like leeches. The boy falls to the floor, bound by the cloth things, unable to see, but still able to breath.

He hears Ursula's plans to keep him in the attic and her threats to turn Lettie inside out.

Lettie doesn't threaten Ursula at all, but uses her real name, Skarthach of the Keep. She asks the creature to consider why there are no others of its kind around and warns of the 'varmints' that come to eat fleas.

Ursula bolts from the house, following the trail of broken toys Lettie had laid out for her.

Lettie tells the boy a story about a flea from Cromwell's time that they managed to get rid of just in time, before the varmints came.

Questions

1. Does the boy get a good night's sleep in the Hempstocks' farmhouse?

2. What does he see when he looks out the window in the middle of the night? How does he feel when he sees this? Comment on how he feels here.

3. Describe the clothes left out for the boy. Do they strike you as unusual?

4. Why does he have difficulty finding the kitchen?

5. Where has Lettie gone, when the boy goes downstairs?

6. Why doesn't Ginnie hate Ursula Monkton? Is there sense in what she says?

7. What do you think will happen next?

8. What does the boy have for breakfast? Does he enjoy this meal?

9. How does Lettie look when she comes in?

10. Lettie tells the boy he doesn't have to go with her while she goes to speak with Ursula. What reason does he give for wanting to go with her? What is Lettie's reaction to this?

11. Describe the scene as they sit by Lettie's ocean.

12.   What do they begin talking about?

13.   What "truth" does Lettie tell the boy?

14.   'You won't let her get me, will you?'
           Why does the boy place such faith in Lettie?
           Would you feel the same way, in his position?

15.   'We don't do spells'
           Does this surprise you?
           What reason does Lettie give for this?

16.   What is the stuff in Lettie's shopping bag for?

17.   Explain what Lettie is doing as she goes around the
           property, depositing broken toys.

18.   "I would have trusted her to the gates of Hell and back"
           Describe the children's friendship.
           Why does he feel like this about Lettie?

19.   What does Lettie say Ursula is doing now?

20.   Describe the scene they find in Ursula Monkton's room.

21.   Why does Ursula think that "this is the best place in the
           whole world"?

22.   Ursula says that she isn't scared of Lettie. What does she
           say that makes us doubt Lettie and her abilities?

23.   Why does the boy find Ursula so scary? Comment on this.

24.   Describe what happens to the grey strips hanging from the ceiling.

25.   What does Ursula threaten to do to Lettie?
        Comment on this image.

26.   How does Lettie frighten Ursula?

27.   "And she's scared. Poor thing."
        Lettie sounds like she feels sorry for Ursula. Does this surprise you?

28.   What are your expectations of the 'varmints' Lettie mentions?
        Do you think they will be something to be scared of?

Chapter XI

Summary

Lettie and the boy find Ursula out on the lawn, struggling to open the jam jar to get out the wormhole inside. She is upset and crying, something that makes the boy uncomfortable as he is not used to seeing adults cry.

Ursula asks Lettie to send her back, afraid of whatever it is that is coming for her.

Lettie opens the jam jar for her and Ursula throws the wormhole onto the grass, where it transforms into a tunnel.

Ursula cannot enter the tunnel as it is incomplete. She turns and focuses on the boy's chest, before grabbing him.

She turns into something part flesh, part rotting canvas and old wood, holding the boy fifteen feet above the ground. Ursula accuses Lettie of blocking the way, which Lettie denies. Lettie asks her to put the boy down.

Ursula insists that her way home is inside the boy and he is certain that he is about to die. Lettie insists that they will still be able to send her home, but Ursula is not convinced. She says she will get away by ripping out the boy's heart.

Lettie tells Ursula she's used up her chances and whistles, summoning black, winged creatures. Lettie asks Ursula to release the boy again.

Ursula makes no move to release him. The hunger birds begin to swoop in and tear her apart, gobbling up her remains.

After they have finished with Ursula Monkton, the black creatures from the sky devour the wormhole too. Then they land, and the boy cannot count or explain their number. They appear as shadows to him.

These creatures tell Lettie that she has no power over them, that they have come to clean, and something still remains for them.

Lettie quickly walks the boy to the fairy ring in his garden and tells him not to leave it, not for anything. Then she runs off.

Questions

1. What emotional state is Ursula Monkton in?
    What does this tell you?

2. Why does Ursula ask Lettie to send her back?

3. Describe what happens when Ursula throws the
    wormhole onto the grass.

4. Why does Ursula stop and wail as she is about to return
    through her tunnel?

5. Why does Ursula unfurl and grab the boy?

6. Describe what Ursula transforms into.

7. Ursula says the way home is inside the boy.
    What is your reaction to this?
    What do you expect her to do?

8. Why does Lettie whistle?

9. Describe the creatures that arrive.

10. "I found myself imagining a valley filled with dinosaurs...."
    Comment on the imagery in this chapter.

11. What do the hunger birds do to Ursula?

12. "...when the screaming stopped, I knew that Ursula
    Monkton was gone for ever."

What is your response to this development?

Is the boy safe now?

13.   Why don't the 'cleaners' leave?

14.   Why does Lettie take the boy to the fairy ring?

15.   Describe the atmosphere at this point.

Chapter XII

Summary

The boy stays inside the fairy ring, terrified, while the shadowy cleaners encircle it. He stays there as the sun dips in the sky and the shadowy shapes grow blurry and indistinct.

The opal miner appears and talks to the boy, telling him to let the cleaners finish up their work. He tells the boy that Lettie cannot save him, that his fate is sealed. The boy recites a poem from *Alice in Wonderland* to himself as a distraction. When he opens his eyes, the dead man is gone.

The boy's sister comes outside, saying their father is on the phone. She wants to know where Ursula is, as she's hungry. The boy is not convinced that she is really his sister, so he stays put in the fairy ring.

Darkness falls. The boy's father comes out to make him come in. His father is annoyed and shouts at him. The boy gets upset and starts to cry. He asks his father if making a little boy cry makes him feel big, and instantly regrets it. His father goes back to the house without setting foot in the fairy ring.

Ursula Monkton appears in the garden, telling him the cleaners have promised him to her, to keep her company in the place inside them.

After Ursula's visit, Lettie Hempstock appears and tells him he can leave, that her Gran has fixed things. He sits down by the dead tree and challenges her to come over if she is really Lettie.

'Lettie' laughs and turns back into a shadow, before telling him he is tired, done, friendless and hated. The voice tells him that Lettie is not coming back, that he can step out of the circle and his pain will end forever.

The voice is no longer a single voice, but a chorus of indeterminate number. It tells him that he will never be happy, that there is a hole in his heart, a gateway to lands beyond his world. It tells him that he will never be fulfilled, that he won't grow and will die with a hole inside him.

The boy replies to the voice, saying that perhaps it will be like that and perhaps it won't. He says that he doesn't care, that he will wait for Lettie to return. He says that if he dies, he will die waiting for Lettie, that it would be a preferable death to being torn apart by the cleaners because he had something inside him that he doesn't even want.

His outburst is met by silence. The boy realises that everything he said was true. He is not afraid of the dark in this moment and is willing to die waiting for his friend.

He waits. Nothing more comes to him or speaks to him from beyond the circle. He sings quietly to himself, glad to remember all the words of the song.

Questions

1. "I have never been as frightened as I was in that grass circle with the dead tree in the centre, on that afternoon." Describe this scene. Is it very tense, in your opinion?

2. What does the opal miner tell him to do?

3. The dead man tells him that Lettie cannot save him. Do you believe him?

4. What does the boy do to distract himself from the dead opal miner?

5. Is it significant that he recites a poem from *Alice In Wonderland*?

6. Why is the boy suspicious of his sister?

7. What makes the boy cry as he waits in the fairy ring?

8. Do you think it was really his father that he spoke to? Explain your view.

9. Describe Ursula Monkton as she appears in the garden.

10. What message does Ursula have for him?
    What is your reaction to this?
    Is this a creepy or scary moment in the story? Explain your response.

11. The boy is not tricked by the shadow that looks like Lettie Hempstock. What does this tell you about him?

12. What does the "voice in the night" tell the boy?
     How is it trying to make him feel?
     How would you react in his position?

13. Why is he determined to wait for Lettie?
     What is your reaction to this?

14. How do you feel as the chapter ends?

15. Is this the darkest moment in the story so far?
     Explain your view.

Chapter XIII

Summary

Lettie returns with a bucket of water, walking straight into the fairy ring, and apologises for taking so long. She explains that she needed her Gran's help as the ocean didn't want to go with her.

Lettie asks him if he was scared and if they tried to lure him out of the circle. She is proud of him for staying put.

Lettie instructs the boy to step into the bucket and he does so, becoming entirely submerged. Lettie holds his hand as he holds his breath, then begins spluttering and gulping in water. To his surprise, he doesn't choke, the water does him no harm at all.

He realises that he knows everything, that Lettie's ocean flows in him and it fills the whole universe. He is still holding Lettie's hand and turns to see she is made of what looks like silken sheets, filled with tiny, flickering candle flames.

The boy wonders how he looks, in the ocean, and realises he could never know this.

He feels he could stay here forever, in this place of knowledge and knowing, but Lettie says he cannot, warning that it would dissolve him, that he would lose himself here.

When he surfaces, he finds himself standing thigh-deep in water in the Hempstocks' duckpond, still holding Lettie's hand.

As he leaves the ocean, his clothes are completely dry and he no longer knows everything. He asks Lettie about this and finds out it is the same for her, she too loses this knowledge when she is Lettie.

Inside, the boy eats shepherd's pie while Lettie speaks with Ginnie about the approaching cleaners. Ginnie is unruffled by their approach, while their numbers have made Lettie anxious. Ginnie says that they'll send them back to where they come from, that they'll sort things out like they always do, but Lettie is not convinced.

The boy misses the kitten, realising he wants to say goodbye to it. He is just beginning to say something about if he has to die that night, when Ginnie interrupts him and tells him that nobody is going to die. Her being an adult reassures him.

He leaves the farmhouse holding Lettie's hand, intent on not letting go.

Questions

1. What took Lettie so long?

2. Describe the water in Lettie's bucket.

3. Why is Lettie proud of the boy?

4. *"I will never let go of your hand, not unless you tell me to."* Comment on the boy's friendship with Lettie.

5. What happens when he steps into Lettie's bucket?

6. "I did not know where I was, or what was happening, but even under the water I could feel that Lettie was still holding my hand." Comment on this image. How does it make you feel?

7. Describe what the boy sees under the water.

8. Describe Lettie, as she appears here. What does her appearance suggest about her?

9. What is the one thing the boy cannot know, in this place of infinite knowledge? Does this make sense to you?

10. The boy feels he could stay in the ocean forever, but Lettie warns against it. Why does she do this?

11. When he surfaces, where does he find himself?

12. What does he lose when he leaves the ocean?
Are you surprised that this is the case for Lettie too?

13. Why is the boy "scared of eating food outside my home..."?
Are you surprised by this? How does this detail add to your understanding of his character?

14. What do Lettie and Ginnie discuss as the boy eats? What is your reaction to Lettie's urgent tone?

15. What does Ginnie compare Ursula Monkton to? Is this a good comparison?

16. The boy thinks he may die later that night as the chapter ends. How do you feel at this point?

Chapter XIV

Summary

Ginnie, Lettie and the boy leave the farmhouse and walk down the lane to the place where the opal miner's body was discovered. Ginnie calls the cleaners to make them come out.

Old Mrs Hempstock is asleep, so she can't help them.

The boy asks Lettie if they could snip out the piece of him that the cleaners want, but Lettie tells him it's too difficult, as it's in his heart.

The hunger birds arrive and settle just outside the farm boundaries. They are large and hungry. The boy finds it hard to describe them, he can't keep their true faces in his head.

Ginnie tells the hunger birds to hop it, and they laugh at her, demanding the boy. They say they do not need to leave until they do what they came for.

Ginnie is unafraid and tells them to go home, with Lettie adding that the boy is protected by their land.

Unable to eat the boy, they begin to eat the world, wolfing it down, leaving a grey void in its place. The boy realises that soon there will be no world left. Knowing this, he lets go of Lettie's hand and runs towards the cleaners before he can change his mind, even though he fears what they will do to him.

Something knocks him down. At this point he has a ghost memory, as if snipped, of the hunger birds tearing open his chest and devouring his heart.

A voice tells him not to move. Lettie is lying on top of him, squashing him into the ground to protect him from the hunger birds. Lettie wails in pain.

Another voice challenges the birds, saying that it is unacceptable that they harm her family. The voice sounds like Old Mrs Hempstock and the hunger birds sound afraid of her. The voice accuses them of violating pacts, laws and treaties, and then there is silence.

Lettie's body is rolled off him and he sees Ginnie Hempstock.

A hunger bird speaks to say they are sorry for her loss.

Old Mrs Hempstock, shining bright and silver, threatens to bind the hunger birds in the heart of a dark star or have them removed from the list of created things. She goes on to say that she'll deal with them in her own way, and they thank her. But first, she says, they must put back everything that they ate when they began to eat the world.

The boy realises that he is humming and holding on to Ginnie. She says that the hunger birds could have hurt the boy and this world and it would have meant nothing, but they have overstepped by hurting Lettie, a Hempstock.

The boy asks if Lettie will be okay, and Ginnie continues to hold him and

Lettie tight, rocking and crooning.

Old Mrs Hempstock tells him that he's safe, that the cleaners won't be back again.

The boy thinks that Lettie is dead, and that it is his fault, but they tell him she's not dead, but ill. Ginnie carries Lettie to the duckpond and places her in the moonlit water. A giant wave comes and crashes over Lettie's floating body.
There is no splash, the pond is still and small, no longer a great ocean, and Lettie is nowhere in sight.

Ginnie Hempstock says she will take him home.

Questions

1. Describe the night as they leave the farmhouse.

2. Why don't they wake up Old Mrs Hempstock?

3. "'Right!' she shouted to the night. 'Let's be having you.'" Does Ginnie Hempstock's approach to this problem surprise you at all?

4. Why won't 'snipping' the problem work this time?

5. Why is it difficult for the boy to describe the hunger birds? Do they sound frightening to you?

6. How do the hunger birds react to Ginnie's order to leave?

7. Is Ginnie scared of these creatures? Do you think she is brave or foolish?

8. How do the hunger birds respond to Ginnie? Are you worried about the boy?

9. *"But we can hurt this one"* What do the hunger birds do to get what they want?

10. Describe the atmosphere at this point.

11. "I let go of Lettie Hempstock's hand and I ran." Why does the boy run towards the hunger birds? What does this tell you about his character? Do you admire him or feel sorry for him here?

12.   Describe his ghost memory.
      What do you think is going on here?

13.   What does Lettie do to save him?

14.   'There are pacts, and there are laws and there are treaties,
      and you have violated all of them.'
      What do Old Mrs Hempstock's words suggest about our
      knowledge of the universe?

15.   How do you know that the cleaners are afraid of Old Mrs
      Hempstock?

16.   "But Lettie's a Hempstock."
      What have the hunger birds done?

17.   What does Ginnie Hempstock's upset tell you?

18.   What did Lettie do for the boy?

19.   Describe Lettie's condition at this point.

20.   Why does the boy apologise?

21.   What does Ginnie Hempstock do with Lettie?

22.   What happens when Ginnie places Lettie in the pond?

23.   How does Old Mrs Hempstock explain what has
      happened to Lettie?

24.   Are you confused as the chapter ends?
      What did you expect to happen?

25.   How do you think the story ends?

Chapter XV

Summary

The boy and Ginnie get into the Hempstocks' Land Rover. He tells her he thinks that Lettie is really dead. Ginnie explains that she's very badly hurt and the ocean has taken her. She doesn't know if it will ever give her back, but says she can hope. He hopes for this too, as hard as he can.

He asks Ginnie questions about her family and learns that Lettie has no father, that Old Mrs Hempstock, Ginnie and Lettie are the pure thing. She says that Hempstock men have fathered babies, but they are not pure.

The boy asks if he can wait on the Hempstock farm for Lettie to come back from the ocean. Ginnie tells him he cannot, that he has to grow up and try to be worth the life Lettie gave him.

The boy resents this advice, feeling that life is hard enough already, without having to wonder if what you do is worth someone's life.

Ginnie rings his doorbell and tells his mother he's back from Lettie's going away party. She says Lettie is going to Australia, to be with her father.

The boy has lost some of his knowledge about what has happened. He feels tired, knowing the party was fun, but not remembering much about it. He knows he won't visit the Hempstock farm again, unless Lettie is there.

His mother, unsurprised by his late arrival home, tells him that Ursula Monkton had to leave due to family reasons. The boy knows he dislikes Ursula, but cannot remember why, and he feels a bit guilty about this. He doesn't return to his old bedroom either, but continues to share with his sister.

The speaker moves forward in time, telling more about his childhood. He tells of how the house was demolished after they moved out five years later, and how as an adult his sister revealed that she suspected Ursula had to leave because their father was having an affair with her. He could have asked his parents about this as both were still alive at the time, but he didn't.

The speaker says that he learned from his father and childhood, not to shout, especially not at children. He says he finally became friends with his father in his twenties, that he thinks his father was disappointed to have a bookish child, so unlike himself.

He recounts that he never went to the end of the lane again, or thought of the white mini, remembering the opal miner as he was when he was alive. Monster, the cat the miner gave him, wandered off to be fed by other families.

About a month after the events of the story, he came home from school one day to find a young cat by the back door. He took her in and fed her, and she became his pet. Because of her unusual eye colour that made him think of the seaside, he called her Ocean.

Questions

1.   What do they talk about as Ginnie Hempstock drives him home?

2.   What is the mood of the story like at this point?

3.   Why won't Ginnie let the boy stay with them?
Do you feel sorry for him here?

4.   What excuse does Ginnie give the boy's mother to explain where he's been?

5.   "The party had been fun, although I could not remember much about it."
What is your reaction to this?

6.   Once he returns home, the speaker fills in lots of additional information about growing up. What do you learn about his house?

7.   Years later, what does his sister confide to him about Ursula Monkton?
Are you surprised by this?

8.   What does the speaker say he learned from his father and childhood? Is this good advice?

9.   "I finally made friends with my father when I entered my twenties."
What is your reaction to this?

10.   Who did the boy find by the back door about a month after the frightening events of the story?

What is your reaction to this?

11.   Is this a good pet for the boy? Explain your view.

Epilogue

Summary

The speaker returns to the present, where his older self sits by the Hempstocks' duckpond. He thinks about his kitten and how he adored her. He can't remember what happened her in the end, but reflects that this doesn't matter, death happens to all of us.

The old woman brings him out a sandwich and a cup of tea. He realises she is Old Mrs Hempstock.

He asks Old Mrs Hempstock if it is all true, meaning his memories, and she tells him it probably is. He also asks her why he came here and she says he wanted to be alone after the funeral, so he came here, like he always does. Although he doesn't remember it, she tells him that he has visited before.

Ginnie arrives and explains his visits as Lettie's way of finding out if what she did for him was worth it.

Ginnie tells him that the hunger birds tore out his heart, but Lettie couldn't stand his screams, she had to do something about it. This isn't how the speaker remembers it.

He asks if he can talk to Lettie, but Ginnie tells him she's sleeping and healing, not talking yet.

He realises Lettie's been examining him as he sat there and asks if he's passed, but Ginnie replies that you can't pass or fail at being a person.

She tells him he's doing better than the last time they saw him, that he has grown a new heart.

He wonders what happens next and she tells him he'll go home, as he always does. He says he doesn't know where home is and she tells him he always says that.

He walks to the pond's edge and thanks Lettie for saving his life. Old Mrs Hempstock remarks that Lettie never should have brought him along at the start of it all, but that she'll learn for the next time.

He asks if he'll come back to them again, but they don't give him an answer. They encourage him to go, as people are wondering where he has got to.

He hears a cat miaow and sees a cat just like his one. Ginnie explains that he returned her to them.

The speaker turns to leave. He has forgotten the events of the past, mentioning Lettie writing from Australia.

As he drives away, he thinks he sees two moons in his rearview mirror. He wonders about it for only a moment, before dismissing the notion altogether.

Questions

1. Where does this chapter begin?

2. What does the speaker mean when he tells the old woman he had sort of fallen into the pond?

3. Are you surprised that he enjoys the sandwich she gives him?

4. How does she explain his reasons for coming to the Hempstock farm that day?
    Does anything in her explanation strike you as odd?

5. Are you surprised to learn that he has visited the Hempstocks over the years?

6. How does Ginnie explain his visit to their farm?

7. 'The hunger birds tore out your heart. You screamed so piteously as you died. She couldn't abide that. She had to do something.'
    What is your reaction to Ginnie Hempstock's version of events?
    What does it tell you about Lettie?
    What does it tell you about friendship?

8. Why can't he talk to Lettie now?

9. What has been happening as the speaker has been sitting on the bench?

10. 'I think you're doing better than you were the last time we saw you. You're growing a new heart, for a start.'
What is your reaction to this?

11. Why does he thank Lettie?

12. What is Old Mrs Hempstock's response to his apology?

13. What do we learn about his cat?

14. As he prepares to leave, what happens to his memory?
Do you find this frustrating?
Does this development fit the story well?

15. What does he see in his rearview mirror as he drives away?

16. Do you think he will ever see Lettie again?

17. Do you like this ending?

18. What questions are you left with?

19. Did you enjoy this novel? Explain your answer.

20. Is the boy a good choice of narrator? Explain.

21. Is the boy a good 'hero'? Explain your view.

22. What view of childhood does this story give?
Use examples to support the points you make.

23. What view of adulthood does this story give? Use examples to support the points you make.

24. What does the author suggest about the world around us, in this story?

25. The speaker never fully discovers the Hempstocks' full story. What do you imagine this story to be? How do you explain their powers?

26. What has the speaker lost in this story? What has he gained?

CLASSROOM QUESTIONS GUIDES

Short books of questions, designed to save teachers time and lead to rewarding classroom experiences.

www.SceneBySceneGuides.com